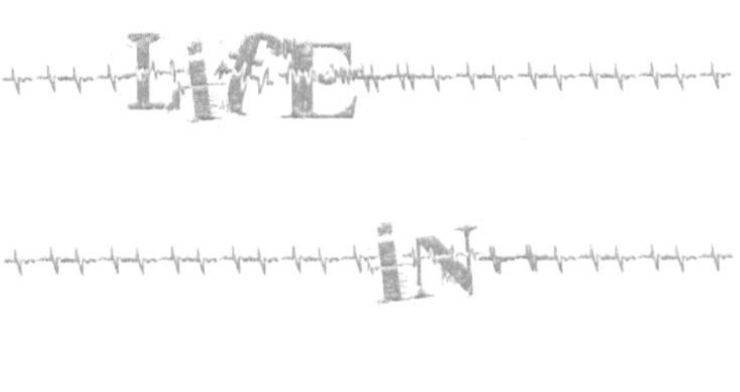
LIFE
IN
VERSES

RL
Literary productions

About the Book

The poems have been written for the author to participate in the Jara Carillo Humor Contest and the 42nd Ciudad de Badajoz Poetry Prize, both in 2023.

Unfortunately, the author was not the winner.

Table of Contents

Silent Witnesses

Like birds, you fly,
Above all and everyone, you pass by.
You spread like veins on all sides,
You are found on all sites.

You pass over houses, fly over trees, and cross rivers,
Wherever we are, we are watched by the wires.
There are no limits to where you can reach,
You are even in the farthest city.

Through your strength, the electricity is running on,
The electricity illuminates life and turns all things on.
Human lives would stop without electricity,
Nothing would work in our daily lives and activities.

Besides electricity, you also bear the information,
You allow the world to keep its communications.
At impressive speed, it happens the transmission,
There is instant communication from Brazil to Japan.

Every day, you accomplish your mission,

Resisting each day and each change of seasons.

You will be there until your last life's day,

The day when the old wiring will be replaced.

Routine

Wake up, eat, exercise,
Take a shower and go to work.
Work, have lunch, and work,
Go back home, take a shower, eat,
Sit down and watch TV.

Sleep a bit and then wake again,
Another day I will begin,
Again, I will get ready,
Repeating everything endlessly.

The routine controls my life,
I do the same thing every day and night.
I cannot see any new thing,
I am in a film repeated on TV.

The film ends and starts one more time,
There is no rest for the mind.
The brain works without thinking,
He knows how to act because of much repeating.

A circle with no end snared me,

There is nothing new for me.

I can only follow what I started,

Wake up, eat, exercise.

Repeat one more time…

Red and Blue

Red and blue, Red and blue, Red and blue.
They are coming, and I don't know what they'll do,
I don't know if they'll come for bad or good,
I know that soon they'll arrive in my neighborhood.

Red and blue, Red and blue, Red and blue.
They arrive and say many things, can I trust them?
They get close, and I don't know what they plan,
They see a black person and start to accuse them.

Red and blue, Red and blue, Red and blue.
They accuse the black without any reason,
They pursue them like they deserve condemnation.
Their rights are not taken into consideration.

Red and blue, Red and blue, Red and blue.
They continue until they arrest the chased one.
The person is treated as an enemy of everyone,
They act as if there are no laws for their actions.

Red and blue, Red and blue, Red and blue.
Another black person was taken from the vicinity,
Another person can be a victim of brutality,
Another person was robbed of their liberty.

Red and blue, Red and blue, Red and blue.
They take innocent people to detention.
And there they will face unfair accusations,
They were just thrown into this situation.

Red and blue, Red and blue, Red and blue.
Violence was exaggerated against that black person,
And they were mowed down.
But this is not the story that will be spread around.

Red and blue, Red and blue, Red and blue.
A lie about what happened will be created,
One that says that other lives were threatened,
And it was worthless that one who is dead…

Chaos

The city does not have police,

At any time of the day, the crime takes place.

The city has no authority,

Each one seeks their wishes.

The city has no ruler over it,

The violence is so alarming.

The city has no legislator,

Fear and panic grow.

The state has no governor,

Everything is going from bad to worse.

The state has no good laws,

Each place established its barons.

The state does not respond to any necessity,

The people live in great inequality.

The state has no justice,

People have neither rights nor peace.

The country does not have a president,

There is no help for its inhabitants.

The country lives in dishonesty,

Nobody talks the truth nor lives correctly.

The country does not have a solution,

Everybody is condemned to destruction.

The country will not last a long time,

In a short moment, everyone will die.

Undesired Changes

I know one season is not forever,

In Earth's cycle, it must change from one to another.

The planet has to pass through transitions,

There are benefits in each of the seasons.

However, I don't like all the alterations,

I don't like winter and fall; sterile and cold seasons.

They produce a very cold and hard time,

During these days, we see only a little light.

In the fall begins the change in appearance,

Nature loses its life and loses its essence.

The trees lose their clothes, their leaves,

I see another world when I look at this.

In the winter there are more changes in the landscape,

Nature talks in a different language and shows another face.

We heard strong winds saying the cold has arrived,

The coldest and darkest weather of the year started.

I look through the window and remember summer days,

Days in which the sun harmed all my ways.

Days in which I could walk freely,

Times when all the people took to the streets.

I miss having one of these days,

If it were possible, I'd only live on summer days.

However, nobody can live like this,

I long for the days when spring will come and hug me.

Hard to Work

I arrive at my office to start working,

I turn on the computer for the action to begin.

I'm ready to perform many tasks,

However, my computer doesn't think like that.

System initialization takes an eternity,

It doesn't look like a computer from modernity.

I feel I'm dealing with equipment from ancient times,

This machine can neither sum nor multiply.

The screen freezes in the Welcome word,

This waiting is making me nervous.

I'm impatient and angry about this situation,

I wanna start my job functions.

Something will happen, there is a change in the screen,

It will start a deep error checking.

This means that will take almost a half day,

Thousands of computer actions, I have to wait.

After wasting a lot of time waiting,

The computer appears to be working.

I'll use it, however, there is another thing,

The antivirus found something.

They stop all my actions,

I must wait for their verifications.

It seems that finally, I can do my work,

The computer is ready to be used.

I open the tools that I'm going to use,

And the computer starts to freeze.

None of the tools works well,

To do something, I need patience at a high level.

I called IT support to get some help,

I'm tired of facing alone this piece of hell.

Someone arrives and checks attentively,

Then he says there is nothing to fix.

He says everything is as it should be,

And there is nothing to do, I just keep waiting.

I'm gentle and thank his attention,

I continue working even in a hard situation.

Little by little, the slowness is improving,

And my work, finally, I'm doing.

I leave the office and feel a failure in the power,

I go back to see the status of my computer.

I look at him with sadness and disillusion,

It has shut down and is on new initialization.

Those Days

How wonderful were those days,

When there were simple all our ways.

We lived freely without any preoccupation,

Our only wish was to have a good diversion.

In the morning, we had to go to school,

And even being there, life was good.

We had some disciplines to study,

There was no risk of failing; all was easy.

There was also a place to meet friends,

A place to establish groups of children.

Groups where everyone felt important,

Groups where nobody got sad or disappointed.

We came back home quickly,

In the cartoon episode, we were thinking.

Everyone saw the same cartoon on television,

And later, this was the topic of the conversation.

Each of us was one of the heroes,

Dreaming about having their powers.

We created infinite imaginary worlds,

Worlds where all conflicts were resolved.

In our minds, there was nothing impossible,

In the imagination, all things were possible.

The whole afternoon we played in the streets,

We played in international sports tournaments.

We were the athletes we watched play,

Dreaming that we would be there one day.

We also spent hours in games and activities,

It was great to play tag or hide-and-seek!

Sometimes the games went into the night,

The mothers came "threatening" our lives.

Everyone was angry with our delay,

The fun didn't let us see hours going away.

We returned to our homes only to take a shower,

Thinking that soon we would have another fun hour.

This was the most important task of our lives,

It was how we lived in childhood times.

Memories

Sometimes, I remember many past things,

I remember many places I have been.

I remember many people I have seen,

I have a huge suitcase of memories.

I miss the streets where I played,

I miss the streets where I walked.

At that time, everything seemed very usual,

Today, I see how everything was special.

I miss the people who lived near me,

It was pleasant; we were almost a family.

Relationships were built with sincerity,

For sure there were some disappointments,

But the sadness endured only for a moment.

It did not take long to reconcile,

Friendship always kept us side by side.

I miss the houses where I lived,
Especially when I pass in those streets.
I remember how I played in that house,
I remember even how my mom cried out.
Each one of these houses brings me emotions,
Each one of them gives me some sensations.

I miss the girls to whom I talked,
I regret not having tried to conquer them.
I was always very close to them,
I knew they would become beautiful women.
At that time, nobody thought about dates,
Everyone just wanted to have fun and play.

Days of the past are always more special,
These days seem to have nothing exceptional.
I desperately wish to go back to that time!
I wish to revive intensely that life!

Ever Present

Wherever there are people, they can see you,

Always waiting for someone to use you.

Some people use you very delicately,

And others, on the contrary, use you very aggressively.

You are used in all kinds of places,

You are very versatile and can be used in a million ways.

You can be used to express something,

Or just to communicate something.

No matter what, people never stop using it.

You are used to expressing various feelings,

Love, hate, forgive, and all that the people are thinking.

You are used when people are sick on a bed,

And also when people are declared healed.

You are used in remarkably formal environments,

And also in extremely casual environments.

The rich use you, but their models are incomparable,

They do not use the same type as all the people.

You can be made of metal, plastic, or another material,

Regardless of what is done, you are essential.

Without you, there would be no agreements,

Great plans would not have any development.

And the whole world would be stopped,

It would lack the crucial for the agreement to be signed.

The pen would be missing, the protagonist of the situation,

Without a pen, no one signs their decision.

They are essential even for the most developed nations,

Without them, everyone would be in great confusion.

Without pens, there would not be annotations,

Who will remember what was said on all occasions?

Without pens, there would be no loving notes,

Not even the sweet words in the vows.

Without them, offices would not have communication,

Because no one could record the information.

I hope the pens never die,

And they always continue in people's lives.

May the pen be always reinvented,

And so, they never stop being used.

Emotions

Sometimes, I see something that raises my fascination,

I look at it and think, "This represents perfection."

I keep looking at it because I like that sensation.

Other times things make me very angry,

I see something, and pretty soon, I'm disgusted.

I'd like that memory to be erased.

There are many things worth of adoration,

Not religious adoration, they deserve appreciation,

It is very good what is before my vision.

And there is that which deserves only disgust,

It causes great revulsion, and I can't even look at it,

There is no way I can accept it.

Other things fulfill my being with desire,

I wish intensely to have it in my life,

I can't have peace till my wish is satisfied.

And many others arouse great fear,

I only imagine them, and I have tremors.

I do my best to never get near.

There are days when I appreciate diversion,

I enjoy each moment of relaxation.

I enjoy what happens in all situations.

Sometimes, the day is full of boring,

There is no good moment on it,

The day drags on in great suffering.

I live some moments with great calm and tranquility,

Everything is wonderful, peace reigns in totality,

I hope to continue living that good reality.

Hopes are ruined by some confusion,

All becomes chaotic and dominated by desperation,

This drives me crazy; I stay without reaction.

There are moments when I'm dominated by sympathy,

I try to be well and share good energy,

I want everyone around me to be happy.

The opposite also happens, and sometimes, I envy,
If I'm not well, I don't want anyone happy,
I do my best to make them as sad as me.

Daily, I see many things and appreciate their beauty,
Especially in nature, there are many beautiful things,
Magnificent and special works with great nobility.

There are also some uncomfortable things,
I look twice to confirm that is really happening,
That should be in darkness; nobody should see it.

My thoughts often come back to the past,
I remember places and people, and what I left,
This seems better than what I have.

My mind also becomes anxious about what will occur,
They don't wanna be here, they wanna the future,
They wanna a new path to go through.

When I look at my wife the desire burns in my heart,
I wanna give her many kisses and hold her in my arms,
I wanna enjoy our passion with a lot of sex.

And there are moments when I feel a painful empathy,
I feel like her pains belong to me,
I do my best to relieve her anguish.

Some things cause me great excitement,
Letting my spirit in great amazement,
I don't wanna still, I wanna make things happen.

I also see things that seem a hallucination,
This deserves a careful investigation,
Because they produced a very frightening sensation.

There are things I just look, and I'm already interested,
It seems like something cool, and I wanna that,
I'm sure it's something I need to have.

I also see things that cause great horror,
I only think, and they already caused me terror,
They produce feelings of pain and discomfort.

Life also brings me many happy days,
I am blessed with good things every day,
There are great wonders in all my ways.

However, there are also sad moments,

Moments in which runs out my strength,

There is no greatness in any instant.

There is always romance with my beloved wife,

We are always enjoying full passion in our lives,

Our house is always full of love and desire.

Now is my time to enjoy the satisfaction,

I have reached the end of this beautiful creation.

I suppose I could express a little of each emotion.

It is a great triumph to be here with you,

I know I tried my best to enchant you,

And I hope it has touched you.

The House of Mind

Mind is like a house with many divisions,
At them live memories, feelings, and emotions.
Each of the rooms has its own appearance,
Each one has its own organization and essence.

Good feelings are in colorful environments,
They use many intense colors; all are vibrant.
Love hugs all those who enter there.
Their great kindness, they always want to share.

Joy awakens smiles and animation,
They always say everyone deserves diversion.
Joy does not let anyone be sad,
If they need to, a joke will be told.

Hope renews everybody.
Saying that everyone must continue cheerfully.
Tenderness treats everyone very kindly.
They want everyone to live very affectionately.

Pride is too satisfied with each job,
They are happy for all that was done.
Gratitude thanks to everyone for visiting them,
"Be grateful for your life," they always recommend.

Negative feelings are in gray places,
It seems dangerous to visit that place.
Fear does not allow anybody to get in,
They see damages and risks in everything.

Sadness welcomes all the people crying.
Without noticing, their visitors are weeping.
Guilt is always very ashamed,
They always think people will criticize them.

Resentment remembers past pains,
They are free but behave like someone in chains.
Envy notices everyone who enters their room,
And all someone has, they want for their possession.

Hate does not even let anyone get inside,

They despise all people and their lives.

They hate everyone for no reason,

No one can approach their room.

One must be careful when walking in their mind's mansion,

There are many doors, ways, and directions.

One must follow vivid and colorful ways,

Those who welcome and treat them like friends.

From Seed to Tree

Everybody's life is always in movement,

Things are happening at all moments.

Human beings will never be totally stopped,

Something is always being developed.

In the womb, a new human being starts to grow,

Their essential functions begin to show.

Their tiny heart gives their first beats,

The parents are amazed when they hear it.

The embryo becomes a baby,

Their body will grow like a seed in a vase.

Soon their parents will see how they will be,

Each new exam increases parents' expectancy.

Parents want to touch this new human being.

The womb becomes small, and the baby must come out,

There is a huge new world they must figure out.

A world where all will be different,

A place to see people and be seen by them.

Parents care for the baby with unconditional love,
They want to protect them from all that is bad.
Their mission is to ensure that they grow well and wise,
Becoming a great man or woman in adult life.

Until achieve maturity, there will be a large way,
First, it will start their childhood days.
They will learn to walk, talk, and express themselves,
They will learn how to communicate well.

The child will forth from their small garden,
They will meet other shoots and plants.
Their life in society will begin,
Many new things will be seen.

Their branches and leaves keep growing,
New marks on their trunk are emerging.
They look at their body and see new things,
They look at another person and have new feelings.

It has begun a new relationship time,
The person has the first love of their life.
They learn how sweet the love can be,
And also what is pain and suffering.

In pain's moment, all seems terrible,
Their recovery seems impossible.
However, the trunk will always regenerate,
Stronger for all storms they will face.

Time does not stop; they learn about responsibility,
Life teaches them that one must face reality.
Their parents will not be here their entire life,
One day, their parents will die.

That little baby became an adult,
The seed became a trunk bold and robust.
Someone strong and brave to face the world.
Someone who will do their best every day,
The main protagonist in their life and ways.

Seeking Wisdom

Life is made of many valuable things,

The wisdom's value is above everything.

It is so valuable that nobody can buy it,

They are like a jewel that people must seek.

All the days, wisdom is at disposition,

One must think carefully before making a decision.

One must know when to be silent,

Words must be said at the right moment.

A restrained tongue will avoid much confusion,

A prudent tongue will avoid many confrontations.

The person must seek wisdom in their work,

Seeking the best ways to apply their efforts.

One also must avoid laziness and negligence,

Working with perfection and diligence.

One can also find it in their driving,

Driving cautiously, gently, and politely.

Avoiding fights and unpleasant situations,

Avoiding irrational behaviors.

Wisdom can be found at home,

Speaking gently with everyone.

Another person will not be angry with a soft tone,

The person must think about the other's reaction.

One must see oneself with another's vision.

Wisdom is within reach and must be attained,

With simple actions, it can be practiced.

Practice will lead one to perfection,

Filling one's heart and mind with wisdom.

Smile

The smile of someone is their main introduction,
A smile completely changes their expression.
A person who sees one smiling can be happy,
The smile conveys that there is music in the air.

Seeing a smile can change a terrible day,
The smiles can show elegance and sympathy.
The one who gains a smile will be infected,
They will smile, giving back the smile they earned.

A sweet smile can change a situation,
Smiling can be a tranquilizer and a solution.
That which was hard and very complicated,
After a smile, it is easy to be made.

The smile has the power to be enchanting,
Some may start a new love after seeing it.
The smile awakens desire and attraction,
A smile can ignite a passion.

Everyone has that power in their smiles,

Everyone should use it all the time.

Don't worry if you don't have the smile you would like,

The most important thing is that you share your smile.

Admiration from a Distance

I long for the moment when I'll see you,
The moment when I'll be close to you.
For me, it's the best hour of my daily life,
It's the moment that I feel alive.
I feel overjoyed at this time.

I get closer and start watching you,
How I would like to be still more close to you!
I can't do it; this is a forbidden relationship,
I can only admire what my eyes can see.

I see you so gorgeous, pretty, and wonderful,
I see your shape, and it's always very beautiful.
My heart beats strong when I think of you,
I dream of the day when I'll be with you.

Sometimes, I think I should give way to my passion,
I should approach you and give in to my temptation.
Something inside me says I have to do it,
I can't hide what I want; I've reached my limit.

I decided today will be a decision day!

All I feel and desire, I'll say.

I took a deep breath and walked towards you,

I feel like I'm going to die, I'm so nervous!

I had no idea; I took you out of the display case,

Very soon someone came to reprimand me:

"Hey, kid! Release it immediately!

I know you can't pay for it! Leave promptly!"

I left the store very quickly,

That tasty cake stayed in my mind.

Will I ever be able to buy it?

Will my hunger ever be satisfied?

Passion

Passion is one of the most beautiful feelings,

They always show themselves with intensity.

The passionate one lives the hurricane of the emotion,

Their heart beat fast with an accelerated respiration.

In their spirit, one has tremendous exaltation.

One gets sad when they are far from their passion,

They do their best to keep that union.

The passionate one wants to live a burning passion,

The object of their desire dwells in their imagination.

Passion can be for a person considered special,

A person that one regards as exceptional.

One admires the person and fulfills their desires,

Without them, one cannot see beauty in their lives.

There are people passionate about their work,

They work at all times without resting hours.

Their tasks are the reason for their existence,

The company is their place of residence.

One can be passionate about their family,

Doing everything to make them happy.

One has no life outside their beloved ones,

Because it is always supporting everyone.

Others are passionate about sports teams,

They live in stadiums to see them playing.

The person lives the team's lives as their own life,

Smiling when they smile and crying when they cry.

Care is necessary in all types of passion,

So that feeling does not become an obsession.

Leaving the passionate one in suffering and tension.

One must balance their passion with moderation,

Then they can be happy and live with satisfaction.

That Too Will Pass

Are you having a hard time in your life?

Don't worry, that too will pass.

Do you think today is the worst day of your life?

Tomorrow will be another day; that too will pass.

Are you living an incredible moment?

Don't get attached to this; that too will pass.

Are you feeling terrible pain?

The pain will go away soon; that too will pass.

Are you experiencing exceptional joy?

Enjoy it fully; that too will pass.

Are you tired of seeing injustice and evil?

Don't be so angry; that too will pass.

Are you very encouraged by the kindness of people?

Don't be too happy; that too will pass.

Did your partner break your heart?

Forget about that person; that too will pass.

Does anxiety for an answer keep you from sleeping?

Relax and sleep; that too will pass.

Does the fear of the future not let you continue?

Face it bravely, that too will pass.

Do the days seem bad and hopeless?

Change your attitude; that too will pass.

Nothing lasts, after all, everything will always pass.

The Weakness

The man believes he is very intelligent and wise,

He always wants to reaffirm the superiority of his mind.

He says that he handles everything with great firmness,

However, every man has a great weakness!

Man is not defeated by another stronger than him,

He is defeated by his "another" head and its wish.

One always surrenders to beauty.

Before a curve, it will go away all his certainties!

He cannot see a beautiful pair of breasts,

And that changes his desires and priorities.

The man cannot resist temptation,

A beautiful woman clouds his judgment and reason.

If he sees a butt and considers it magnificent,

He stares at it for a moment.

He loses his natural sense in front of that,

To animal behavior, he comes back.

Motivation to Work

I arrive at my work and try to do it with devotion,
I bring within me great motivation:
I have many debts that I have to pay.
So there is no option but to work every day.

If it depended on my will, I wouldn't work,
Here, all the day I'm hurt by many thorns.
In this job, there is always confusion and mess,
There is always someone testing my goodness.

One comes and says a ton of meaningless things,
Another comes and tells me their whole history.
Oh, my God! It's tough to hear this all the time!
I endure everything and still have to smile.

This is the painful life of most of the nation,
Everyone stands it for the same reason:
Everyone works hard to survive.
Nobody wants to have a homeless life.

The Price of Dream

I was anxious to start my own company,

I desired another life; I didn't wanna be an employee.

Becoming an entrepreneur, it was my wish,

But before that, I had to fight against bureaucracy.

I melted down when I knew all I had to prepare,

To get everything, I would have to run everywhere.

There is no easy way for those who are starting,

The government is like a great wall blocking me.

I went to a government office with many documents,

They didn't even look at me and said, "Wait a moment."

I waited until someone desired to work,

And I prayed to God for them to grant me their favor.

It's very usual for them to say that is lacking something,

If that happens, I get out of my mind and get angry.

I was tired of waiting and said, "I'm waiting for someone!"

They responded, "We'll analyze your petition."

This simple moment became an eternity,

I couldn't stand with my usual tranquility,

My anguish increased and became affliction,

And to get worse, nobody provided any information.

After a long wait, someone called me,

Finally, something would succeed.

The person analyzed all my documentation,

I was very attentive to each expression.

For me, this was a moment of great tension,

Sweat, dry mouth, and heart acceleration.

The person was satisfied with what had seen,

And they said the registration process would begin.

I could breathe relief! Thank God!

Now, it's the hardest part: my register being approved.

I must await the office's reply to me,

While I'm waiting, I continue with my life and dreams.

I know the government is busy, and this will take time,

However, there is no pause in citizen's lives.

Possible Dreams

Every day the world introduces to us some novelty,
We see wonderful things to make people happy.
The world enchants us with everything that is produced,
All people are amazed at the dreams that are sold.

It is sold the dream of a sculptural body,
You'll have perfect abs instead of a big belly.
You'll get a desirable and wonderful body,
All the people around will see it and envy it!
Like a Greek god, you'll be worshiped.

You have to do only one thing for this to take place,
It's very irrelevant, practically a piece of cake.
A very powerful formula you are going to buy,
Your body is going to be sculpted magically.
There is no risk; you can trust blindly…

We also see the dream of ultra-fast fortune,
You will have millions of bills instantly!
Money will come to you quite magically.
You won't have to get tired or upset your mind,
Very soon, you'll have a prosperous life.

Change your life; join our group of investments,
With us, your return is astonishing.
You'll relax from this very moment,
Trust us, and your money will never stop growing,
There is no chance of anything bad happening!

You can also buy the dream of personal power,
You can even declare your death's hour!
You'll access a power that is hidden from everyone.
You'll be above all human conventions.
You'll stop being a nobody and become someone.

Start today your process of transformation!
Gather with those who are ready to be victorious.
Get out of your conformity and resignation!
Reborn in your higher form; be glorious,
Everything is possible through payment and contribution…

You can have your own company,

You won't have to work constantly.

You can be the boss and owner of your life.

You can decide how much you will work.

And you will still have many bonuses and perks.

Come to a meeting and discover how to get liberty,

Learn how to be the leader you were born to be.

Learn how to unleash your potential and change reality.

Be willing to climb the pyramid and keep rising.

Be willing to open your mind and wallet immediately…

Mighty Smells

Sometimes, I go to some bathrooms and get hit,

It is very stinky; it seems like something has died.

If I stay in that place, I will faint.

If I don't get out quickly, I don't know if I'll survive.

I don't know what someone ate to cause this destruction,

Not even the garbage smell raises this sensation.

I think one needs an investigation,

If they don't get well, death will give them an invitation.

If it's lethal while alive, what will happen when they die?

It's so hard to endure them being still alive,

I think the earth will spit them out when they die.

About the Author

Rafael Henrique dos Santos Lima

Associate Degree in Administration and M.B.A. in Strategic Project Management by Centro Universitário UNA. Christian by the grace of God. Passionate about writing (English, Portuguese, Spanish), poet and novelist.

Contacts

rafael50001@hotmail.com

rafaelhsts@gmail.com

Blog: escritorrafaellima.blogspot.com

Acknowledgements

The following sites contain a lot of useful information for the translation.

Bing AI

Google Docs

Google Translator

Grammarly

Language Tool

Oxford Dictionary

Rhyme Zone

Special Acknowledgement

I thank God. He gave me the intelligence to write the poems.